# ESKIMO BOY

Life in an Inupiaq Eskimo Village

Written and photographed by Russ Kendall

 **SCHOLASTIC INC.** * *NEW YORK*

# Acknowledgments

My deepest thanks and appreciation to all those who helped make this book a reality.

To Norman Kokeok; his parents, Clara and Shelton; his brothers, John and Warren; his sister, Frieda; and his grandmother, Signa. To Dawn Weyiouanna, my first friend in Alaska; her husband, Dick; and their son, Bradley. To Stella Weyiouanna and her children, Andrew and Peter, the big and little Goobers. To Easu Weyiouanna, the village elder who shared many truths about Eskimo life with me and who gave me my Eskimo name. To Clifford Weyiouanna, who taught me how not to herd reindeer. To John Sinnok, who helped me with the Glossary. To all the other good and generous children and adults of Shishmaref, and to all the teachers at the village school who put up with my songs and with my questions. To Gary at Perfecta Camera, in New Hampshire, who sent me an emergency box of film from 6,000 miles away. To my editor, Dianne Hess, for her patience, encouragement, and wisdom. To my parents, both sets, Jean and Jim Carson, and Bonnie and Russ Kendall. And to Thérèse for all else.

A NOTE ABOUT THE BOOK: While preparing the text for publication, every effort was made to be sensitive to and respectful of the Native Alaskan cultures and languages. Concerned about the term "Eskimo," several authorities, who are Native Alaskan, were questioned. We found that in Alaska, where our book takes place, the term is commonly used among the native people who do not find it offensive. They do, however, greatly appreciate acknowledgment of specific Alaskan cultures, for example, Inupiaq, Yup'ik, etc.

*Library of Congress Cataloging-in-Publication Data*

Kendall, Russ.
Eskimo boy / written and photographed by Russ Kendall.
p.  cm.
Summary: A photo-essay describing the village, customs, and traditions of an Eskimo boy living in Alaska.
1. Eskimos—Alaska—Juvenile literature.  [1. Eskimos—Alaska.
2. Indians of North America—Alaska.]  I. Title.
E99.E7K42  1991                          90-9157
979.8'004971—dc20                        CIP
ISBN 0-590-43695-3

                                    AC
12 11 10 9 8 7 6 5 4 3 2 1    1 2 3 4 5 6/9
                                    36

Printed in the U.S.A.

First Scholastic printing, March 1992

Designed by Marijka Kostiw

# Dedication

*This book is dedicated to Owen Burke, who taught me that educating one's self is a lifelong endeavor that goes far beyond the pages of our textbooks.*

This is Norman Kokeok. He is a seven-year-old
Inupiaq Eskimo. In the Inupiaq language, the word
"Inupiaq" (in-OO-pee-ak) means "the real people."
Let's look at where he lives.

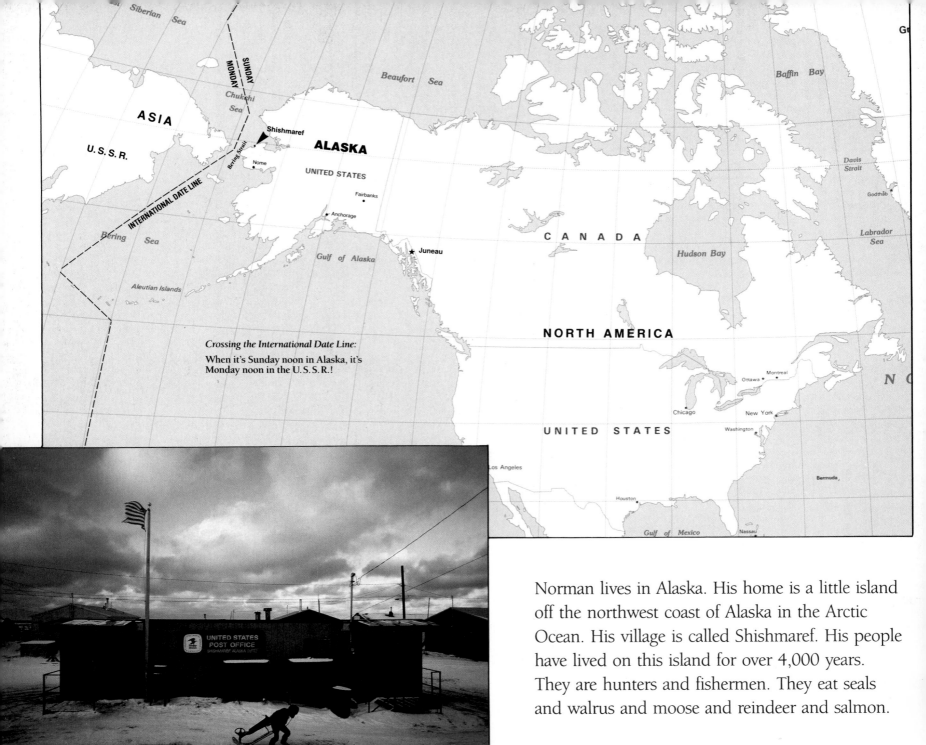

ASIA

U.S.S.R.

SUNDAY MONDAY

Chukchi Sea

Siberian Sea

Shishmaref

ALASKA

Nome

UNITED STATES

Fairbanks

Anchorage

Bering Strait

INTERNATIONAL DATE LINE

Bering Sea

Gulf of Alaska

Juneau

Aleutian Islands

Beaufort Sea

Baffin Bay

Davis Strait

Godthåb

Labrador Sea

CANADA

Hudson Bay

NORTH AMERICA

Ottawa

Montreal

Chicago

New York

UNITED STATES

Washington

Bermuda

Houston

Gulf of Mexico

Nassau

Los Angeles

*Crossing the International Date Line:*

When it's Sunday noon in Alaska, it's
Monday noon in the U.S.S.R.!

UNITED STATES POST OFFICE
SHISHMAREF ALASKA 99772

Norman lives in Alaska. His home is a little island
off the northwest coast of Alaska in the Arctic
Ocean. His village is called Shishmaref. His people
have lived on this island for over 4,000 years.
They are hunters and fishermen. They eat seals
and walrus and moose and reindeer and salmon.

Eskimos in Alaska don't live in igloos. They
live in houses.

*Warren*

*Frieda*

Norman's brother, Warren, is twenty-three years old. He has his own family, and they live in a small house on the other side of the village. His sister, Frieda, is twenty-one, and his brother, John, is

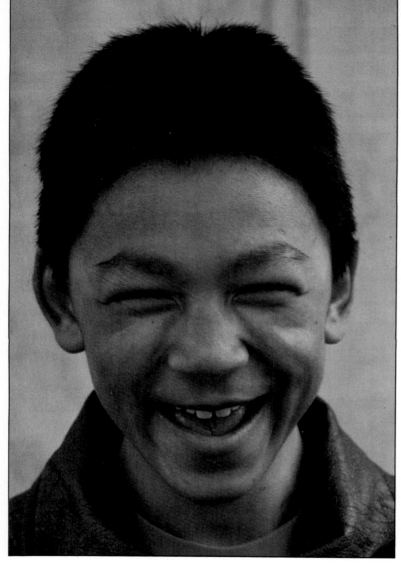

*John*

*Clara and Shelton Kokeok*

*Norman and his grandmother, Signa*

thirteen. Norman's parents are Clara and Shelton Kokeok. His grandmother, Signa, lives nearby in her own house.

Winter comes early to Shishmaref. Sometimes it snows in September. As the temperature gets colder, the nights get longer. In the middle of winter there is only one hour of daylight, and the thermometer can go down to 65 degrees below zero. It gets so cold that the whole ocean freezes! During storms, the wind can blow more than one hundred miles per hour.

If you walk out on the ice for several miles and then turn around, you can see Ear Mountain rising up behind the village. Though it looks close, it is almost thirty miles from the island, across the water on the mainland.

When it is really cold and dark, the northern lights come out. If you look up in the sky you can see them stretching far into the distance, like ribbons moving and flickering, glowing green and red.

Norman's grandmother has told him that if he whistles at them, they might come down to earth and glow even brighter. But then he must be careful, she tells him, because if they come too low, they might try to snatch his head and play with it!

You can see a group of stars in the sky called the Big Dipper. The Big Dipper is on the Alaska state flag.

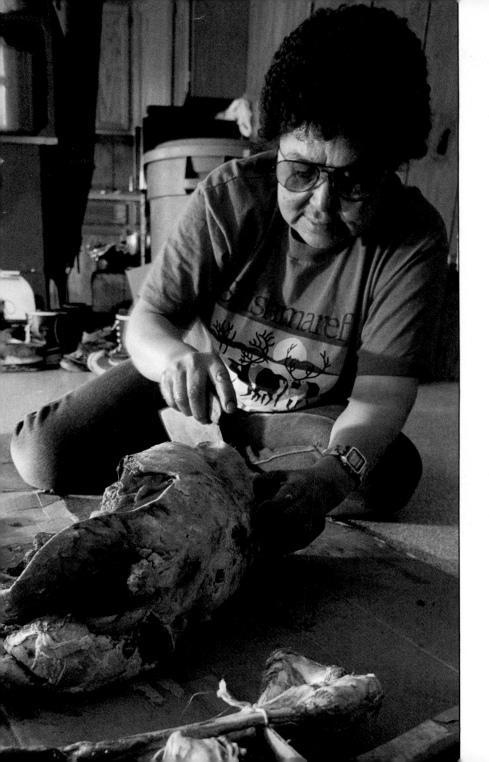

Norman's father is a hunter. Whenever he catches something, he brings it home, where Norman's mother cleans and prepares it. She cooks some of the food right away; the rest she dries or freezes and saves for later. She uses an "ulu," or women's knife, to cut the meat or the fish.

13

Norman is not old enough to go on the hunt with the men from the village. But he dreams of being a great hunter. For now, his favorite activity is going ice fishing with other villagers out on the frozen lagoon that separates the island from the mainland.

About 450 Inupiaq Eskimos live in Shishmaref. There are only a few white people, mostly teachers who work in the village school.

Norman is in the first grade. He would rather be outside fishing, but he tries to do well in school. Sometimes he gets frustrated, especially when he has to read.

His teacher, Dawn Weyiouanna, has taught

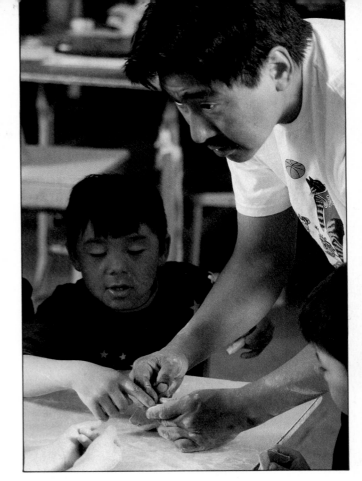

the class to say the Pledge of Allegiance in sign language. Some days the class watches videotapes about animals like polar bears, which sometimes come into the village at night in the winter. Other days, they learn how to speak the Inupiaq language and how to carve little people and little animals out of soapstone. The carving teacher, Dick Weyiouanna, carves animals from walrus ivory.

Before the white man came to Alaska, the only way to travel was to ride a dogsled. Today, Eskimos use snow machines to travel and to hunt. But most families still ride dogsleds for fun and sometimes to race.

There are almost as many dogs in Shishmaref as there are people. Even when it gets very cold, the dogs live outside. Their fur keeps them warm. Sometimes the men make their dogs hot meals by boiling water and fat and seal meat and fish together.

Because the village of Shishmaref is so far north, no roads go there. But there is a runway nearby where airplanes can land. Almost everything that comes into or goes out of the village is brought on airplanes. Norman's parents take him, by plane, to the dentist in Nome, 120 miles away. He is not very happy to go.

The village does not have running water. Norman's parents travel to the Alaskan mainland where they chop ice from a small pond. Then they bring it back to the island and melt it for drinking water.

In the spring the days begin to get longer again. Shishmaref holds a spring carnival. People from other Eskimo villages all over Alaska come to help celebrate the longer days. Outside there are dogsled races. Inside the school, there are basketball games, and later there are Eskimo dances. The dancers dance to the beat of a big, thin Eskimo drum. After the carnival, Norman and some friends play Eskimo baseball in the snow.

In May, the snow that covers the island begins to melt. In June, the village becomes full of big slush puddles. People drive their snow machines right through the water. The ice pack that covers the ocean begins to break up and melt and drift away.

Soon the men will begin hunting seals and walrus so the village will have enough food for the next winter. Even though Norman cannot go with the men, he watches them leave, then pretends to shoot at seals from the shore. When the men bring seals back, the village women clean them, then hang up long strips of seal meat to dry in the wind.

In the summer there is almost no ice or snow left. The sun stays up most of the time, setting for only one hour each night. While the men are away hunting and fishing, the village children play outside. Norman especially likes to play near the ocean. He watches the boats leave the island as the hunters go to their hunting and fishing camps.

Norman and his friend Andrew practice hunting near the airplane runway where many birds live. When he shoots one with the BB gun his father gave him, he brings it to his grandmother as is the village custom. She cleans and cooks it for him. Norman wants to be as good a hunter as his father. Someday Norman will use these hunting skills to feed his family.

Too soon the brief Arctic summer is over. Norman knows he must soon return to school, this time to the second grade.

The cold September winds have already
started blowing. Soon they will carry winter
snowstorms. The nights are already getting
longer and colder. In a month's time, the
ocean will begin to freeze. Norman puts on
his winter parka and, missing summer
already, walks down to the ocean.

# Inupiaq Eskimo Words

Aana (AHN * aa) . . . . . . . . . . grandmother

Aniu (ah * NEE * oo) . . . . . . . snow

Ataata (a * DAH * ta) . . . . . . father

Ava (AH * va) . . . . . . . . . . grandfather

Iglu (IG * loo) . . . . . . . . . . snow house

Ini (IN * ee) . . . . . . . . . . . wood or sod house

Inupiaq (in * OO * pee * ak) . . . . the real people

Kammak (COME * muck) . . . . . sealskin boots

Kiugzat (kee * YOG * zaht) . . . . northern lights

Mazaq (MA * zuck) . . . . . . . sun

Nanuq (nun * OOK) . . . . . . . polar bear

Qayaq (KUY * ack) . . . . . . . small, skin-covered boat

Qimugun (KEE * moo * gun) . . . . dog

Sauzaq (SEW * zuck) . . . . . . . Eskimo drum

Tagiuq (TA * gee * uk) . . . . . . ocean

Taqiq (TA * kick) . . . . . . . . moon

Ugzruk (OOG * zrook) . . . . . . bearded seal

Uiviilaak (oo * EE * vee * lok) . . . babies

Ulu (OO * loo) . . . . . . . . . women's knife

Umiaq (OO * mee * ack) . . . . . large boat

Uniat (OO * nee * aht) . . . . . . dogsled

# AFTERWORD

## Modern-day Eskimos

There are about 40,000 Native Alaskans in Alaska. Inupiaq Eskimos, like Norman and his village, make up only one Native Alaskan culture. There are many others, each with its own history, traditions, and language. There are the Aleuts, who live on the Aleutian Islands of southwestern Alaska; the Athabascans of interior Alaska; the Yup'iks, who live along the west coast; the Tlingits and Haidas of the southeastern panhandle; and others.

It is thought that the first Eskimos came to North America from Asia, crossing the frozen Bering Strait into western Alaska, between 4,000 and 6,000 years ago. Some say they might have been following herds of caribou. Anthropologists have found ancient artifacts on and near Shishmaref that are estimated to be that old. Because Eskimos had no written language until the mid-1900s, there are no written records of those prehistoric times. But small hand tools, dolls, and carvings found in archaeological digs closely resemble hand tools, dolls, and carvings used and produced, until recently, by modern Eskimos. Over the centuries, the nomadic Eskimos spread east and south, migrating thousands of miles along the coast of North America, through Canada and as far Northeast as Greenland. A few thousand Inupiaq Eskimos still live in Siberia.

American Indians are thought to be the product of a similar, but much earlier, migration. Their ancestors crossed over from Asia between 25,000 and 40,000 years ago, then migrated south and east, inhabiting all of North and South America.

Modern-day Eskimos are in a precarious place. Though they have lived in Alaska for thousands of years, they now find themselves strangers in their own land, strangers to their own culture. A gentle, trusting people, they proved easy prey, first for the Russian whalers and hunters who exploited and enslaved them in the 1800s, and then for the Americans who came throughout the 1900s, looking first for gold and then for oil.

Eskimos had no concept of land ownership or of a cash economy. The land, and the sea, provided them with everything they needed. Food was shared according to need. Tools, boats, and even dogs were shared almost to the point of collective ownership. There had been no need for money or private property for 4,000 years. All that changed with the advent of the white man.

In the 1940s and 1950s, white schools and churches were built in remote villages. The Eskimo children, who were forced to attend them, were more and more taught the white man's ways at the expense of their own. Eskimo children were punished and hit with sticks if they spoke their native tongue while in school or church. Stores began to appear in the same villages, and a subsistence economy gave way to a cash economy. White men, who had been housed and fed by Eskimos, began selling them food and alcohol, and later, guns and snow machines. Eskimos, who were traditionally very healthy, began to contract and suffer, even die from, white man's diseases: alcoholism, tobacco addiction, tooth decay, suicide, etc.

When Alaska was admitted to the union as the forty-ninth state in 1959, the accelerated influx of the white influence further diluted the Eskimo culture. Some villages, in an effort to protect themselves that went completely against their cultural generosity, began making white men unwelcome. Some, like Shishmaref, were far enough away from the white man's centers of commerce and population that the cultural collision was not as great as it was in other villages.

In the space of three generations, entire tribal cultures were either wiped out or irrevocably altered. There are cases where grandparents, who speak only their native tongue, cannot speak with their own grandchildren, who speak only English.

As older native speakers of these languages die, they are replaced by younger Eskimos who speak mostly English, who themselves are eventually replaced by still younger Eskimos who speak only English. Large pieces of the culture are lost forever. Norman, who can speak and understand a great deal of the Inupiaq language, is more the exception than the rule. His parents are older than those of his classmates and closer to "the old ways" than some of the younger parents who are themselves a product of the white man's school system, which teaches English at the expense of Inupiaq, wood shop at the expense of hunting skills. But there are those Eskimos who are fighting the loss of their heritage, some of whom are college-educated and return to their villages to study and relearn the old ways so they can teach them to the young ones. Some schools are beginning to teach "bilingual" classes, where carving, language, and Eskimo values are taught alongside American history and math. Much of the hope for future generations of Eskimos to rediscover their rich heritage lies with these Native Alaskan leaders.

## About Alaska

Alaska is about one-fifth the size of the rest of the United States. If you superimposed Alaska over the lower forty-eight states, the southern end of the panhandle would be in Florida, the western end of the Aleutian Islands would be in southern California, and the northern edge of the state would touch Canada.

The U.S.S.R., which is only about sixty miles to the west, across the narrow Bering Strait, declared territorial ownership of Alaska in the late 1700s, but sold it to the United States in 1867 for $7,200,000. That works out to about two cents an acre.

Everything about Alaska is big. With over 500,000 square miles, it is the largest state. But with only 550,000 people, it is also the least populous. Tiny Rhode Island, with only a little over 1,000 square miles, has twice as many people. In fact, you could put the entire state of Rhode Island inside just the city limits of Anchorage and still have enough room left over for half of the state of Delaware.

Nearly half the population of Alaska, 225,000 people, live in Anchorage. Next comes Fairbanks, with almost 31,000 people. Juneau, the state capital, is third with about 26,000 people. The rest of the residents are scattered throughout the state.

The highest mountain in North America, Denali (Mount McKinley), which is 20,320 feet high, is in central Alaska. Most of the active volcanoes in North America are in Alaska. Mount Redoubt, a volcano near Anchorage, erupted in December of 1989, shutting down air traffic for days and blanketing the city with ash and pumice. A violent and destructive earthquake took place in Alaska on Good Friday, 1964, destroying much of Anchorage.

## About the Photos

The photographs were taken mostly with Nikon equipment. I brought two FM2 bodies and an F4 body with me. For lenses, I used a 20mm f/2.8, a 50mm f/1.8, a 180mm f/2.8, and a Tamron 300mm f/2.8. For some of the very long shots, I used a 2X converter with the 300mm lens.

Notably, the large photo on page 10 was intended to be a four-hour time exposure showing the movement of the stars in the sky, taken with the 20mm lens and the F4, left outside in −20°F weather. Completely by surprise, the aurora appeared during the last four minutes of the exposure! The pictures were taken almost entirely with Kodachrome 64 or 200 film.